The Golfer's Little Instruction Book

The Golfer's Little Instruction Book

Sandy Parr

Thorsons

An Imprint of HarperCollins*Publishers*

Thorsons
An Imprint of HarperCollins*Publishers*
77–85 Fulham Palace Road
Hammersmith, London W6 8JB

Published by Thorsons 1996
3 5 7 9 10 8 6 4 2

© Sandy Parr 1996

Cartoons by Mike Gordon

Sandy Parr asserts the moral right to
be identified as the author of this work

A catalogue record for this book
is available from the British Library

ISBN 0 7225 3376 4

Printed and bound in Great Britain by
Caledonian International Book Manufacturing Ltd, Glasgow

To Bernie Ragger, my regular golfing partner,
and other long-playing members of the
Fifty Club Golfing Society

Introduction

There are many definitions of golf but my own particular favourite describes it as 'A lot of walking broken up by disappointment and bad arithmetic.' Anyone who has been bitten by the golf bug can identify with the second sentiment while the third will strike a chord with reluctant scorers who have been tasked with calculating the winner of the Club Stableford competition.

I can claim to have been an irregular golfer for a good 25 years and hardly an outing goes by without a threat to give up the game completely or a solemn promise that I will go to the driving range at least twice a week. Golf seems to induce such wild emotional fluctuations and mood swings that it sounds strange to hear it described as a hobby. Expectations are always high but results usually disappoint. Perhaps what we need is a little straightforward instruction.

The task of writing several hundred *bons mots* about the game was initially quite daunting. Hasn't it all been said before? I turned to my library of golf books and searched hopefully for some enlightenment. I found acres of print devoted to analysing and dissecting the swing from every conceivable angle, complex solutions for hooking, slicing, shanking and pulling, and even a complete lifestyle guide to help sort out the mental side of the game. But where had all the fun gone?

I hope this selection of golfing wisdom gives a more balanced view of the game. There are some serious points of instruction as well as some more flippant suggestions. Even if you take away only a few ideas to practise and bring into your game, I feel the exercise will have been worthwhile. Enjoy your golf and don't let it get the better of you.

Sandy Parr – April 1996

Author's Note:

The book assumes that all golfers are right-handed men. This is obviously a false assumption so please make the necessary adjustments if you do not conform to this stereotype.

Golf is...

A game to be enjoyed – if you can't enjoy it, you shouldn't be playing.

One of the few games where the better you play, the less you see of the ball.

A game of two halves, 'out' and 'in'.

Like a love affair – if you take it too seriously, it will break your heart.

A game where the player invariably lies better than the ball.

A simple game complicated by the people who play it.

A lot of walking broken up by disappointment and bad arithmetic.

The perfect excuse for adults to carry on playing with expensive toys.

A puzzle without an answer. If you knew the secret, you would be selling it, not playing it.

A playground for perfectionists, pedants and masochists.

Pool played on a larger table.

An expensive way of playing marbles.

Like sex, something you can enjoy without being particularly good at it.

It's in the Bag

Every club has its sweet spot – it's your job to find it.

A good golfer never blames his clubs for a bad shot.

But the great thing about blaming your clubs is that they can't defend themselves.

- Make sure you get the right thickness of grips to suit the size of your hands.

- And aim to replace your grips at least every two years.

- When choosing a set of clubs, try them before you buy them.

Make sure that the clubs suit your physique.

If you're wearing holes in your golf glove, it's telling you something about your grip.

Try to wash your grips on a regular basis. Worn-out grips produce tired shots.

A tartan putter cover is the golfing equivalent of hanging furry dice on your rear-view mirror.

Carry a copy of the *Rules of Golf* in your bag as disputes are inevitable.

A set of waterproofs is an essential part of a golfer's wardrobe – unless you actually enjoy playing in the rain.

Golf umbrellas are fine on the golf course but very anti-social when held dripping wet in a crowded commuter train.

Woolly headcovers will protect your woods and keep your feet warm in bed in the winter.

Baseball caps are on a par with visors and should be banished from the golf course.

If you can't wiggle your toes around in your golf shoes, they are either a size too small or you are standing too far away from the ball.

Fore Play

Good golf is like good sex – the pleasure lies more in the foreplay than the actual scoring.

When gripping the club, the 'Vs' formed by your thumb and forefinger should point at your right shoulder.

Your grip of the club should be firm and light but not squeezed tight.

- Make sure you can see at least two knuckles in your left-hand grip.

- If you have a bad grip, you don't want a good swing.

- A good set-up position is the most important prerequisite for any swing.

A good grip is like shaking hands with the club.

Your stance for the driver should be as wide as your shoulders, and should get narrower as the clubs get shorter.

When addressing the ball, try to release any tension in your elbows and shoulders.

Think of the left arm as the controller and the right arm as the power base.

Take time to develop your own pre-shot routine.

King of the Swingers

The golf swing, like any successful relationship, is largely a matter of trust.

Whatever path your swing has taken, the clubface must be square at impact.

Think of the swing as hands, arms, hips and legs working in unison.

- Concentrate on making a body turn, not a shoulder dip.

- Don't 'hit' from the top of your backswing.

- Hit *through* rather than *at* the ball.

- If you want to know the path your swing has taken, look at your divot pattern.

What you want in the golf swing is a feeling of controlled aggression.

Try to find a tempo that suits your own temperament.

The pace of your swing should feel the same on the way down as it did on the way back.

Swing as easily with the driver as you would with a wedge.

Try hitting some balls with your knees and feet together to get a better feel of the downswing.

Hit some shots with your eyes closed to get the true feeling of the swing.

On the Tee

Before teeing off, swing two clubs together to get your golfing muscles into shape.

Be warned: out-of-bounds is as bad as it sounds.

If there's out-of-bounds on the right, tee up on the right and hit your drive out left.

⊛ It's tough in the rough so keep your ball on the fairway.

⊛ Always use a tee, even on short par-3s. Why throw away an advantage?

⊛ Do long drivers have bigger balls? Or is it just the way they swing?

Follow a proper warm-up routine, even on hot days.

Tee the ball up high for distance, low for accuracy.

Don't leave your best drives on the practice ground.

The woods are full of long drivers.

It is one of the unwritten laws of golf that your practice swing is always better than the one you actually use to hit the ball (this applies especially to your opening drive).

Remember that you hit the ball further by hitting it better, not harder.

On the Beach

A bunker shot is the only shot in golf when you don't have to hit the ball.

When playing from a bunker, keep just one thought in mind – getting out in one shot.

Always rake bunkers behind you. And don't nick the rakes.

Rakes should usually be left outside bunkers, not in the sand.

Vary the distance you hit your bunker shots by varying the amount of sand you take with the ball. More sand for the shorter shots, a cleaner hit for the longer ones.

Keep the clubface open throughout the swing.

When playing out of wet sand, try a 9-iron instead of a sand wedge.

Don't ground your club at address.

Your body should be aimed to the left of the hole and the clubface aimed at the hole.

Keep your wrists firm during the shot.

Think positively when your ball lands in the sand and avoid getting yourself into a bunker mentality.

A fairway bunker shot should always be hit like a normal short iron, with the emphasis on striking the ball as cleanly as possible.

On the Green

A four-foot putt counts the same as a 250-yard drive.

Keep your balls dry in wet weather.

With short putts, concentrate on the line.

With long putts, concentrate on distance.

⊛ Place your marker behind the ball, not in front of it.

⊛ Pitchmarks can be repaired on your putting line, spikemarks can't.

⊛ There's no such thing as a free putt – always get in the habit of holing out.

Don't be afraid to strike short putts firmly into the cup.

When studying a green, don't just look for the contours, but study the grass, and in particular which direction it is lying.

On a links course, bear in mind that the greens usually slope towards the sea.

On an undulating green, try to leave yourself with an uphill putt.

If you've got two putts to win, take them.

Your worst putt is usually better than your best chip.

Don't lean on your putter when you pick the ball out of the hole. Not only could it damage the green, it could also prove embarrassing if you lose your balance.

Whatever your putting style, keep your head still during the stroke.

Calculate the length of your putts in units of 10 feet. That way, if you do occasionally hole a long one, it sounds more impressive in the bar afterwards.

Confidence on the green comes from being able to read the line of your putt.

Handy Hints

You can always hear a good shot.

Never try to correct a fault with another fault.

If you make allowances for a hook or a slice, they'll only take advantage of you.

Your sand wedge is not just for getting out of the sand. It can also be your best pitching club.

When chipping onto the green, get the ball rolling quickly like a putt.

From an uphill or downhill lie, let your swing follow the slope.

Never rush in to play out of trouble.

The secret of missing any hazard is to aim straight at it.

If you can't get out of the rough with a long iron, try a wedge and go for position rather than distance.

Once you've made your selection, let the club do the work.

With the wedge, try to find the right ball position in your stance that gives a consistent height and length of shot.

Always carry a lofted wood in your bag. It will usually be more reliable than a long iron.

On a testing course, make sure you have an adequate supply of balls.

Best Practice

Practice does not make perfect, but it helps.

The more you practise, the 'luckier' you get.

The practice ground is the place where golfers go to convert a nasty hook into a wicked slice.

Don't groove your faults on the driving range. There's plenty of time to do that on the course.

⊛ Limit yourself to a maximum of 40 practice balls in an hour, and take a number of practice swings before each shot.

⊛ Always aim at a target and keep varying your distance.

⊛ Try starting out with a 9-iron and work up through the bag.

Occasionally use a video camera to record your swing and watch how you're progressing on screen.

Concentrate on getting your technique right; the results come later.

Be realistic – expect to hit some bad shots.

Have the confidence to take your practice game onto the course.

If you receive some good advice, write it down and keep referring to it when you practise.

One good practice swing is better than two or three that are different.

Practice helps to put brains in your muscles.

Be honest about the strengths and weaknesses of your game. And don't just practise your strengths.

Squeezing a squash ball is a good way to strengthen the hands and wrists for golf.

Practising your putting in the office is the sign of a misspent career.

Mark your practice balls with your initials if you don't want them confused with anybody else's.

Consistency can only be achieved through knowledge, patience and practice.

Course Strategy

When in doubt take one club more than you think you need.

Know how far you hit the ball with each club.

Scoring is all about getting the ball into the hole in the fewest number of strokes.

Try to finish your round with a par. It will keep you coming back for more.

When playing golf during the week, tell your colleagues that you're on a course.

When asked what course it was, say it was course management.

Discover your favourite pitching distance and aim to leave yourself with an approach shot of that length to the green.

On a course with narrow fairways, it's better to leave your driver in the bag. Or better still, at home.

⊛ Take a 2- or 3-wood off the tee for better positioning and only marginally less distance than a driver.

⊛ Work out how many greens you hit in regulation during a round and try to beat that figure next time you play.

Invest in a yardage chart when you play a new course and take some of the guesswork out of your game.

Don't fight the wind – use it to help shape your shots.

On a long par-4, lay up with your second shot rather than straining to hit the green in two.

Don't change your game to suit the course.

If you're playing on your own, challenge yourself to see how many birdies and pars you can score.

Or see how many times you can get up and down from around the green.

Head to Head

In competition, there's a time to play safe and a time to attack.

Always agree what you're playing for before you start.

And don't play for more than you can afford to lose.

When playing foursomes, always try to keep your partner in play.

A golfer who can chip and putt is a match for anybody. A golfer who cannot is a match for nobody.

Don't be influenced by the club selection of your opponent.

Beware the sick golfer – like his health, he can go round under par.

Don't try to outhit a long hitter.

Forget about your opponent. Play against par.

Golf is a game where you can always find someone to beat and someone who will beat you.

A friendship should never be allowed to interfere with winning a golf game.

Strokeplay is a test of golf but matchplay is a test of character.

Always check the Local Rules on the back of the scorecard before you tee off at an unfamiliar course.

Mind Games

Over-instruction can lead to paralysis through analysis.

Try to visualize each shot before you play it.

The most important distance in golf is the distance between the ears.

- Be prepared to handle bad breaks when they come along – they always will.

- Accept both good and bad luck as integral parts of the game.

- Focus on playing the game; everything else will look after itself.

Don't play the shot up ahead of you until you have played the one in front of you.

Don't let a tough course psych you out before you start.

Only keep one swing thought in your mind at a time.

Don't let one or two bad holes ruin the entire round.

When asked your handicap, don't reply 'my swing'.

The moment you think you've cracked the game, it sneaks up and mugs you.

If you play golf as a form of relaxation, how do you ever manage to work?

You can learn as much from a bad round as you can from a good one.

Always remember that it's great to be outdoors doing something you enjoy.

Play the shot you know you can play, not the one you see played on television by the professionals.

Don't take your problems with you onto the course.

The more confident you are of your game, the better you will play.

A Question of Etiquette

Golf is one of the few sports left where etiquette still matters.

Pitchmarks and divots can ruin a game – always repair them.

Be ready to play when it's your turn.

Avoid unnecessary practice swings and waggles.

If you accidentally drive into the game in front of you, feign amazement that you could actually hit the ball that far.

When arriving at the green to putt, put your clubs down at the most convenient point for the next tee.

Move off smartly to the next tee after holing out.

Don't mark your card on the green.

Don't litter the course, even with broken tee pegs.

⊕   Never take a divot on the teeing area when you make a practice swing.

⊕   Always offer to hold the flagstick when your partner is putting, and be clear whether he wants it tended or removed.

Don't always be the fourth person in your foursome to buy a round.

While your opponent is preparing to putt, don't start practising your own stroke or lining up your shot. At best it's a distraction, at worst it smacks of gamesmanship.

If your opponent concedes a putt, pick up the ball and walk away. If you insist on putting out and miss, don't expect another concession.

If you're getting pressed by a match behind you, let them through and then speed up.

Golfing Lore

In golf it's not 'how' but 'how many' that counts.

You're never too old or too good to learn something new about the game.

Never be afraid to seek advice from a pro.

Take your tips from the pro, not from a friend and certainly not from an opponent.

A husband should never try to teach his wife to play golf or drive a car.

A wife should never try to teach her husband anything. Most are beyond tuition.

Birdies can be common but an eagle and an albatross are extremely rare birds.

Don't let a bad round spoil a good walk.

An old golfer never dies, he just loses his balls.

A bad day on the course still beats a good day in the office.

There's no such thing as bad weather for a dedicated golfer.

A well-adjusted person is someone who can play golf as if it were only a game.

Women play the game but men know the score (or vice versa, depending on which way you dress).

Real golfers go to work to relax.

Nothing goes down slower than a golfer's handicap.

Every shot in golf gives somebody pleasure, even if it's only your opponent.

Always play to the best of your ability.

If you can't break 80, you have no business playing golf.

If you can break 80, you have no business.

A Little Wisdom

Don't forget to pack a hip flask in your bag in winter.

Take out some golf insurance, especially if you are an inveterate slicer or hooker.

Plan to arrive a quarter of an hour before your tee-off time.

Always keep your clubs in the boot of the car. You never know when you might be able to fit in a round.

There's a big difference between watching the ball and staring at it. Don't let that little white ball send you into a trance.

In wet weather, remember to pack a spare glove and a towel to dry your grips.

Having a window sticker in your car that reads 'If you think I'm a bad driver, you ought to see me putt' can count against you if you have to make a claim on your motor insurance policy.

As Christmas approaches, let it be known that you're not in the market for another multi-coloured golf sweater.

If you must cheat at golf, Microsoft Golf will grant you any number of mulligans and gimmes.

Don't leave your clubs unattended outside the clubhouse, even at the smartest of clubs.

Be a golden retriever – watch every shot with an eagle eye.

If you had to take just one golf book to a desert island, make it *Harvey Penick's Little Red Book*.

Don't underestimate how expensive a hobby golf can be.

A dog makes a good golfing companion, especially if you can teach it to find lost balls.

Don't believe the line about the golf course being the best place to do business. It's a myth put about by senior executives who fancy a day out of the office.

More than a Game

The 19th hole is full of golf bores – don't be one of them.

A dream golf course is one that has a halfway house which serves bacon sandwiches and hot toddies. And not just at weekends.

Don't forget to tip the club barman. Otherwise you might find he can be a right bar steward.

Take a golf holiday in Ireland. It has the best courses, the friendliest people and, of course, real draught Guinness.

A pint of Pimms is a fine drink to consider after a hot afternoon's golf, especially if your partner is giving you a lift home.

Glossary (in no particular order)

BABU (Australian expression) – Bloody Awful
but Bloody Useful shot

Blondie (drive off the tee) – A good fair crack up
the middle

Honeymoon shot (usually played to a dog-leg) –
One that opens up the hole

Slapper (drive off the tee) – You wouldn't take it
   back but it's nothing to brag about

That's gone without a forwarding address (to a
   ball hit a long way out of bounds)

On the dance floor but a long way from the
   music (to a putt on the green but not
   threatening the hole)

Texas wedge – Large money clip

Duck hook – A threat to all pond life

Brassie – A bold and fearless hooker

Relief – Permission to pee

Casual water – The result of the above

Lateral water hazard – A fourball relief

Dropping zone (for Members only) – Area
between the men's and ladies' tees after a drive
from the former has failed to reach the latter

Outside Agency (at work) – If you ever manage a
hole-in-one

Burrowing animals – Moles, rabbits, stoats, ferrets, ground hogs etc. i.e. any animal that can be blamed for your lost ball

GUR – The groundsman's attempt to frighten off the above

Hitting it Fat – Swinging like Craig Stadler

Skins game – A midnight dare after closing time

Rub of the Green – When you stop playing golf and start scoring

Observer – Someone who catches you in the act

Press – As in 'we'll be pressing charges'